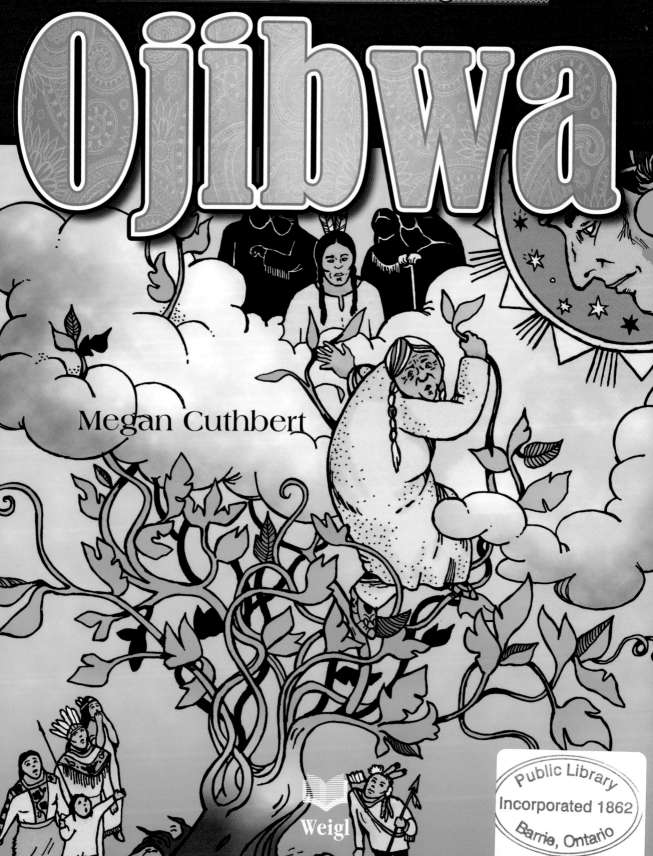

Aboriginal Legends of Canada

Ojibwa

Megan Cuthbert

Weigl

Published by Weigl Educational Publishers Limited
6325 10th Street SE
Calgary, Alberta T2H 2Z9
Website: www.weigl.ca

Library and Archives Canada Cataloguing in Publication
Cuthbert, Megan, 1984-, author
     Ojibwa / Megan Cuthbert.
(Aboriginal legends of Canada)
Issued also in electronic format.
ISBN 978-1-77071-304-8 (bound).--ISBN 978-1-77071-305-5 (pbk.).--
ISBN 978-1-77071-306-2 (ebook)
     1. Ojibwa Indians--Folklore. I. Title.
E99.C6C94 2013   j398.2089'97333   C2013-907328-0
                                                                C2013-907329-9

Printed in the United States of America in North Mankato, Minnesota
1 2 3 4 5 6 7 8 9 0 18 17 16 15 14

062014
WEP110614

Editor: Heather Kissock and Jared Siemens
Design: Mandy Christiansen
Illustrator: Martha Jablonski-Jones

Photo Credits
Weigl acknowledges Getty Images and Alamy as its primary image suppliers for this title.

We acknowledge the financial support of the Government of Canada through the Canada Book Fund for our publishing activities.

CONTENTS

Meet the Ojibwa

The Ojibwa are one of Canada's **Aboriginal** groups. The Ojibwa of the past were hunter-gatherers. They hunted, fished, and gathered berries and plants. The Ojibwa used to live and travel together in groups of 150 to 300 people called bands. These bands lived in parts of Ontario, Manitoba, and Saskatchewan. Today, there are about 140,000 Ojibwa living throughout Canada. Some live in cities, while others live on **reserves**.

Storytelling plays an important role in the life of the Ojibwa. In the past, they used storytelling to help keep Ojibwa bands connected. They told their **legends** through spoken word, song, and dance. Today, the Ojibwa continue to use storytelling to share their **traditions** and history.

Stories of Creation

The Ojibwa creation story is one of the oldest stories told by the Ojibwa. This ancient cultural legend explains where the Ojibwa believe they came from. The Ojibwa tell these stories of creation to new generations to make sure their past is not forgotten.

The Ojibwa call themselves Anishinaabe. This means "original people" in their language.

The Ojibwa believe that the world and all its creatures were made by the creator, Gitchi-Manitou. Gitchi-Manitou is very powerful. In the creation story, the people disappoint Gitchi-Manitou, and he punishes them by sending a great flood to Earth. Everyone must then work together to create a new home for themselves.

Long ago, the Ojibwa lived in dome-shaped houses called wigwams. Wigwam is another word for dwelling.

Muskrats and turtles play a significant role in the Ojibwa creation story.

The CREATION

Long after Gitchi-Manitou created Earth's first people, they began to fight with one another. Gitchi-Manitou decided to make Earth peaceful again by sending down a great flood.

The water covered the whole Earth. All of the people died, except for Nanabush. Almost all of the animals died as well. Nanabush survived by floating on a log. He shared the log with the surviving animals. Nanabush decided he had to make a new land for the animals to live on. He and the animals began diving into the water in search of dirt. None of them had any luck. Then, Muskrat dove deep into the water. He was gone so long that Nanabush and the animals believed he had died. When he finally emerged, Muskrat held a ball of dirt in his paw.

Nanabush took the ball of dirt and spread it on Turtle's back. With the help of Gitchi-Manitou, the dirt grew until it became North America. To this day, the turtle and muskrat are given a good life because of the sacrifice they made for Earth and its people.

Nature Stories

Storytelling is one way the Ojibwa explain the seasons and cycles of nature. Nature played an important role in the Ojibwa's traditional way of life. In the past, the Ojibwa depended on nature for their food, clothing, and homes. This meant they had to pay close attention to the **natural world** and the changes that came with the seasons.

The Messenger of Spring is a story about changing seasons. Long ago, it was important for the Ojibwa to know when spring was coming, because they often **migrated** as the weather changed. In the story, winter leaves Earth a sign that promises new life.

Ojibwa legend says that blooming flowers are an important sign that winter is over.

Birch trees provided the Ojibwa with materials for many practical items. In warm weather, the Ojibwa travelled by birchbark canoe. Wooden snowshoes helped them travel in the winter.

The MESSENGER of SPRING

A long time ago, the world was covered with snow and ice. Suddenly, New Dawn arrived, bringing colour and life to the Earth. Snow melted around him, and grass grew at his feet. The world became green and full of life again.

New Dawn sang a song that warmed the Sun. His song brought animals out of hiding, and made the trees and flowers bloom.

As the world began to change, New Dawn met Iceman. Iceman was the spirit who once ruled over Earth. Iceman was old and tired. He was ready to leave the world he created. As Iceman faded away, he left behind the gift of a flower called Spring Beauty. Spring Beauty became a yearly sign that winter had faded and the new dawn of spring had taken its place.

Life Lessons

The Ojibwa tell stories to teach lessons and important beliefs to their children. Adults and **elders** often use stories to teach children how to behave and treat one another. Stories help make life lessons fun, entertaining, and easy to remember. The Ojibwa tell their stories **orally**, as well as through music and dance.

Traditionally, Ojibwa elders were responsible for teaching children about the values and beliefs of the Ojibwa.

Ladder to the Sky is an Ojibwa tale that teaches about fairness and kindness. It also shows the importance of obeying rules. When an old woman goes against the rules set by Gitchi-Manitou, she finds out how difficult life can become.

Before the Ojibwa had a written language, they recorded their stories by painting pictographs, or picture symbols, onto stone.

Stories told through music and dancing at powwows help teach Ojibwa children about cultural values and traditions.

LADDER to the SKY

L ong ago, Gitchi-Manitou worked hard to keep his people healthy. No one was ever sick, and no one died. When people grew old, Gitchi-Manitou had his spirit messengers bring people up to the sky on a magic vine. These people lived with Gitchi-Manitou and watched over their families below. Only the messengers were allowed to touch and use the vine.

The messengers often came down the vine to check on the people. One day, they found a group of people treating a young man badly. For his protection, the messengers brought the young man up the vine. This upset the young man's grandmother. She climbed up the vine after him. The vine was not strong enough, and she and the vine fell to the earth.

People began to feel pain because of the old woman's disobedience. Some people even died. Gitchi-Manitou wanted to help them get well again. He sent messengers down to teach people how to use plants as medicine to ease their pain. They soon felt better again.

Heroic Tales

Many Ojibwa stories feature heroes and heroines. Sometimes, these heroes go on adventures and face many challenges. One of the most popular Ojibwa heroes is Nanabush. Nanabush often displays both good and bad human **traits**. This makes him a hero to which almost every Ojibwa can relate.

Why People Do Not Live Forever is an Ojibwa story that shows the importance of courage and trust. When Nanabush is sent on a long journey, he encounters a difficult choice. The way he handles the situation affects his people forever.

In one Ojibwa tale, Nanabush transforms into a rabbit to trick a selfish man into sharing his fire.

The Nanabush Trails on the southeastern tip of Lake Simcoe in Ontario were developed to teach people about Ojibwa traditions and history.

Why PEOPLE Do Not Live FOREVER

After making a new home for himself and the animals, Nanabush spent many years wandering Earth alone. He felt restless and unhappy. One night, he heard the voice of Gitchi-Manitou. The voice told Nanabush to walk east until he reached a swift-flowing river. Gitchi-Manitou promised a reward if Nanabush walked across the river.

In the morning, Nanabush began walking east until he found the swift-flowing river. Nanabush was afraid to cross it. Suddenly, he saw a beautiful woman on the other side of the river. Nanabush waded across the river to the woman. The woman told him that Gitchi-Manitou had sent her to be his wife. They wed, and their children became the first Ojibwa people. Nanabush never aged, but his children and grandchildren grew old and died. This was because Nanabush hesitated before crossing the river. He had doubted the word of Gitchi-Manitou.

Activity

Write your own nature legend.

Have you ever wondered why caribou have antlers or why skunks smell so bad? Aboriginal people often tell stories to explain why animals have certain traits. Write a legend of your own by completing the following activity.

You will need:

a piece of paper   a pencil

1. Think about some of the animals in the world. Which features or behaviours make them unique? Is there one animal that really interests you? Make this animal the main character in your legend.

2. Now, think about how your animal came to have this unique feature or behaviour. You may have to add other characters to your legend to explain what happened.

3. Write an outline of your legend. The outline should show what is going to happen in your legend from beginning to end.

4. Take time to review your outline when it is complete. Does the story clearly explain what happened to the animal? Rework the outline until the legend is clear.

5. Once the outline is ready, begin writing your legend. When you are done, read it aloud to your friends and family.

Further Research

Many books and websites provide information on Aboriginal legends. To learn more about this topic, borrow books from the library, or search the internet.

Books

Most libraries have computers that connect to a database for researching information. If you input a key word, you will be provided with a list of books in the library that contain information on that topic. Nonfiction books are arranged numerically, using their call number. Fiction books are organized alphabetically by the author's last name.

Websites

Learn more about the Ojibwa people at: www.thecanadianencyclopedia.com/en/article/ojibwa/

Discover more tales about Ojibwa hero Nanabush at: http://nanabush.ca/

Key Words

Aboriginal: the First Nations, Inuit, and Métis of Canada

elders: the wise people of a community

legends: stories that have been passed down from generation to generation

migrated: moved from one place to another

natural world: relating to things that have not been made by people

orally: by spoken word

reserves: land set aside for First Nations

traditions: established practices and beliefs

traits: qualities or characteristics

Index